First World War
and Army of Occupation
War Diary
France, Belgium and Germany

15 DIVISION
Divisional Troops
Divisional Ammunition Column
3 July 1915 - 30 May 1919

WO95/1924/4

The Naval & Military Press Ltd
www.nmarchive.com
Published in association with The National Archives

Published by

The Naval & Military Press Ltd

Unit 10 Ridgewood Industrial Park,

Uckfield, East Sussex,

TN22 5QE England

Tel: +44 (0) 1825 749494

www.naval-military-press.com

www.nmarchive.com

This diary has been reprinted in facsimile from the original. Any imperfections are inevitably reproduced and the quality may fall short of modern type and cartographic standards.

© Crown Copyright
Images reproduced by permission of The National Archives, London, England, 2015.

Contents

Document type	Place/Title	Date From	Date To
Heading	WO95/1924/4		
Heading	15th Division 15th Divl Ammn Column Jly 1915-May 1919		
Heading	War Diary of 15th Divisional Ammtn Column 1st January 1917-31st January 1917. Volume 13		
Heading	15th Division 70th Brigade ammunition Column Vol: I.		
War Diary	Bulford	07/07/1915	17/07/1915
Heading	15th Division 15th D.A.C. Vol I July to Oct 15		
War Diary	Bulford	03/07/1915	10/07/1915
War Diary	France	11/07/1915	25/09/1915
War Diary	Pommier	00/10/1915	00/10/1915
Heading	15th D.A.C. Vols. 2.3.		
Miscellaneous			
Heading	War Diary 15th Div. Amm. Col. Jany-Dec 1916		
Heading	15th. D.A.C. Vol. 4 Train 16		
War Diary		31/10/1916	31/10/1916
Heading	15th D.A.C. Vol 5		
Miscellaneous			
Heading	15 D.A.C. Vol 6		
Miscellaneous	D.A.C. 3 Echelon	02/06/1916	02/06/1916
War Diary			
Miscellaneous	15 D.A.C. June 1916.	30/06/1916	30/06/1916
War Diary		02/06/1916	23/06/1916
Heading	War Diary 15th D.A.C. From 1st to 31st July. 1916.		
War Diary	Verquigneul	09/07/1916	23/07/1916
War Diary	Wavrans	26/07/1916	26/07/1916
War Diary	Vacquerie Le Boucq	27/07/1916	27/07/1916
War Diary	Mezerolles	28/07/1916	28/07/1916
War Diary	Boisbergues	31/07/1916	31/07/1916
Heading	15th Divisional Artillery. 15th Divisional Ammunition Column R.F.A. August 1916		
Heading	War Diary of 15th Divisional Amtn Column From 1st August 1916 to 31st August, 1916. Volume Dumber 8		
Miscellaneous	The A.G.s Office At Base.	31/08/1916	31/08/1916
War Diary	Bourdon	01/08/1916	01/08/1916
War Diary	Bavelincourt	02/08/1916	02/08/1916
War Diary	La Vieville	03/08/1916	03/08/1916
War Diary	Albert	04/08/1916	04/08/1916
War Diary	Mezerolles.	27/07/1916	27/07/1916
War Diary	Lavieville	14/08/1916	31/08/1916
Heading	War Diary of 15th Div. Ammtn Column. From 1st September, 1916 to 30th September, 1916. Volume Number 9		
Miscellaneous	D.A.C. Office at Base	01/10/1916	01/10/1916
War Diary	Lavieville	03/09/1916	28/09/1916
Heading	War Diary of 15th D.A.C. 1st October, 1916. to 31st October, 1916. Volume. 10		
Miscellaneous	Confidential War Diary of 15th D.A.C. 1-31 October 16 Volume X	31/10/1916	31/10/1916
War Diary	St Gratien	02/10/1916	08/10/1916

Type	Place	From	To
War Diary	Beccurt	15/10/1916	29/10/1916
Miscellaneous	The Officer i/c A.G's Office at the Base	29/11/1916	29/11/1916
Heading	War Diary. of 15th Div Amtn Col From 1st November, 1916-30th November, 1916. Volume 11		
War Diary	Becourt.	07/11/1916	27/11/1916
Heading	War Diary of 15th D.A. Column. From 1st December, 1916 to 31st December, 1916. Volume 12	01/12/1916	01/12/1916
Miscellaneous	To Also Office At Base	31/12/1916	31/12/1916
War Diary	Becourt	02/12/1916	12/12/1916
War Diary	Lavieville	16/12/1916	16/12/1916
War Diary	Lavieville	03/01/1917	29/01/1917
Miscellaneous	To. D.A.G. Base	31/01/1917	31/01/1917
Heading	War Diary of 15th. Divisional Ammunition Column for Month Of February 1917. Volume XX		
Miscellaneous	D.A.G. Base.	28/02/1917	28/02/1917
War Diary	Lavieville	29/01/1917	08/02/1917
War Diary	St. Gratien	09/02/1917	16/02/1917
War Diary	Hem	17/02/1917	17/02/1917
War Diary	Conchy.	18/02/1917	18/02/1917
War Diary	Lavieville	01/02/1917	01/02/1917
War Diary	St Michel	20/02/1917	20/02/1917
War Diary	St Gratien	13/02/1917	13/02/1917
Heading	War Diary of 1st D.A.C. From 1st March 1917-To 31st March 1917 Volume XV		
Miscellaneous	15 D.A. for AG at Base.	31/03/1917	31/03/1917
War Diary	St. Michel	06/03/1917	08/03/1917
War Diary	Habarcq	12/03/1917	27/03/1917
War Diary	Duisans	29/03/1917	29/03/1917
Heading	War Diary of 15th D.A.C. Volume 22 From 1st April 1917. 30th April. 1917.		
War Diary	Duisans	31/03/1917	10/04/1917
War Diary	Arras	11/04/1917	28/04/1917
Miscellaneous	The A.G.S. Office at Base	01/05/1917	01/05/1917
Heading	War Diary of 15th Divisional Ammunition Column. From 1st May. 1917. to 31st May, 1917. (Volume 5).		
Miscellaneous	The A.G.S Office at Base	31/05/1917	31/05/1917
War Diary	Arras	09/05/1917	24/05/1917
War Diary	Habarcq	25/05/1917	25/05/1917
War Diary	Etree Wamin	26/05/1917	26/05/1917
War Diary	Ambromeiz	29/05/1917	29/05/1917
Heading	War Diary of 15th Divisional Ammunition Column From 1st June, 1917. To 30th June 1917. Volume 6. Vol. 21		
Miscellaneous	To A.G.s. Office at Base	01/06/1917	01/06/1917
War Diary	Aubrometz	07/06/1917	16/06/1917
War Diary	Bergueneuse	17/06/1917	17/06/1917
War Diary	St Hilaire	18/06/1917	18/06/1917
War Diary	Steenbecque	20/06/1917	20/06/1917
War Diary	Eecke A.A.	21/06/1917	21/06/1917
War Diary	Watou	24/06/1917	29/06/1917
Heading	War Diary of 15th Divisional Ammunition Colum (Volume7) From 1st July 1917. To 31st July 1917.		
War Diary	Brandhoek	01/07/1917	26/07/1917
War Diary	Brandhoek	18/07/1917	27/07/1917

Heading	War Diary of 15th Divisional Ammunition Column From 1st August 1917. To 31st August 1917. (Volume 8).		
Miscellaneous	The AG's Office at Base		
Miscellaneous	D.A.Gs. Office At Base	31/08/1917	31/08/1917
War Diary	Brandhoek	03/08/1917	30/08/1917
War Diary	Brandhoek	29/08/1917	30/08/1917
Heading	War Diary of 15th Divisional Ammunition Column (Volume 9). From 1/9/17. To 30/9/17		
Miscellaneous	The D.A.C. Base G.H.Q. 3rd Echelon	01/10/1917	01/10/1917
War Diary	Watou	02/09/1917	02/09/1917
War Diary	Cassell	04/09/1917	04/09/1917
War Diary	Esquelbeeque	04/09/1917	04/09/1917
War Diary	Noyellette	06/09/1917	07/09/1917
War Diary	Arras.	14/09/1917	14/09/1917
War Diary	Arras	01/07/1917	20/09/1917
War Diary	Arras	10/09/1917	10/09/1917
War Diary	Arras	01/09/1917	01/09/1917
War Diary	Ligny St Flochel	23/09/1917	23/09/1917
War Diary	Arras.	21/09/1917	28/09/1917
Heading	War Diary of 15th Divisional Ammunition Column From 1st October 1917. To 31st October, 1917. (Volume 10).		
Miscellaneous	To A.G.s. Office Base		
War Diary	Arras.	05/10/1917	24/10/1917
Heading	War Diary of 15th Divisional Ammunition Column (Volume 11) From 1st November 1917. To 30th November 1917.		
Miscellaneous	The A.G.s. Office at Base	01/11/1917	30/11/1917
War Diary	Arras.	04/11/1917	24/11/1917
War Diary	Arras	16/11/1917	17/11/1917
Heading	War Diary of 15th Divisional Ammunition Column. (Volume 12.) From 1st December 1917. To 31st December 1917.		
Miscellaneous	The A.G's Office at Base	31/12/1917	31/12/1917
War Diary	Arras	04/12/1917	30/12/1917
Heading	War Diary of 15th Divisional Ammunition Column (Volume. 13) From 1st January 1918 To 31st January 1918.		
War Diary	Arras	03/01/1918	28/01/1918
Heading	War Diary of 15th Divisional Ammunition Column Volume 14. From 1st February 1918 To 1st March 1918.		
War Diary	Arras	01/02/1918	23/02/1918
Heading	15th Divisional Artillery. 15th Divisional Ammunition Column R.F.A. March 1918		
Heading	War Diary of 15th Divisional Ammunition Column (Volume 15) From 1st March 1918. to 31st March 1918.		
War Diary	Arras	01/03/1918	09/03/1918
Heading	15th Divisional Artillery War Diary 15th Divisional Ammunition Column April 1918		
Heading	War Diary of 15th Divisional Ammunition Column. (Volume 16). From 1st April 1918. To 30th April 1918.		
War Diary	Duisans	03/04/1918	06/04/1918
War Diary	Habarcq	14/04/1918	19/04/1918
War Diary	Monitenter Court	19/04/1918	19/04/1918

War Diary	Habarcq	09/04/1918	09/04/1918
War Diary	Montenescourt	24/04/1918	24/04/1918
Heading	War Diary of 15th Divisional Ammunition Column. (Volume 17.) From 1st May 1918. To 31st May 1918.		
War Diary	Montenescourt	01/05/1918	04/05/1918
War Diary	Anzin	09/05/1918	10/05/1918
War Diary	Maroeuil	18/05/1918	28/05/1918
Heading	War Diary of 15th Divisional Ammunition Column. (Volume 18) From 1st June 1918. To 30th June 1918.		
War Diary	Maroeuil	06/06/1918	23/06/1918
Heading	War Diary of 15th Divisional Ammunition Column. (Volume 19) From 1st July 1918. To 31st July 1918.		
War Diary	Gouves	07/07/1918	15/07/1918
War Diary	Frevin Capelle	16/07/1918	16/07/1918
War Diary	Saly Le Grand	19/07/1918	19/07/1918
War Diary	Verberie	20/07/1918	20/07/1918
War Diary	Vieux Moulin	21/07/1918	21/07/1918
War Diary	Retheuil	22/07/1918	22/07/1918
War Diary	Retheuil	17/07/1918	30/07/1918
Heading	War Diary of 15th Divisional Ammunition Column. From 1st August 1918. To 31st August 1918. (Volume 20).		
War Diary	Soucy	01/08/1918	04/08/1918
War Diary	Chamant	05/08/1918	05/08/1918
War Diary	Sarron	06/08/1918	07/08/1918
War Diary	Magnicourt	09/08/1918	17/08/1918
War Diary	Montenescourt	20/08/1918	27/08/1918
War Diary	Agny.	28/08/1918	28/08/1918
Heading	War Diary of 15th Divisional Ammunition Column. (Volume 21) From 1st September 1918. To 30th September 1918.		
War Diary		01/09/1918	30/09/1918
War Diary		15/09/1918	27/09/1918
Heading	War Diary of 15th D.A.C. From 1/10/18 to 31/15/18 Volume 22. Vol. 37		
War Diary	Barlin	03/10/1918	04/10/1918
War Diary	Bracquemont	07/10/1918	16/10/1918
War Diary	Fosse 7 Loos	17/10/1918	17/10/1918
War Diary	Meurchin	18/10/1918	18/10/1918
War Diary	Carvin	19/10/1918	19/10/1918
War Diary	Wahagnies	20/10/1918	20/10/1918
War Diary	Merignies	21/10/1918	21/10/1918
War Diary	Huquinville	23/10/1918	25/10/1918
War Diary	Genech	28/10/1918	29/10/1918
Heading	War Diary of 15th Divisional Ammunition Column (Volume 23.) From 1st November 1918. To 30th November 1918.		
War Diary	Genach	01/11/1918	08/11/1918
War Diary	Cobrieux	09/11/1918	09/11/1918
War Diary	Le Glanerie	10/11/1918	10/11/1918
War Diary	Wez Velvain	11/11/1918	11/11/1918
War Diary	Baugnies	17/11/1918	27/11/1918
Heading	War Diary of 15th Divisional Ammunition Column. (Volume 24.) From 1st December 1918. To 31st December 1918.		
War Diary	Baugnies.	01/12/1918	16/12/1918

War Diary	Tongre-N-D	17/12/1918	17/12/1918
War Diary	Horrues	18/12/1918	18/12/1918
War Diary	Quenast	20/12/1918	27/12/1918
Heading	War Diary of 15th Divisional Ammunition Column (Volume 25) From 1st January 1919. To 31st January 1919.		
War Diary	Quenast	01/01/1919	28/01/1919
Heading	War Diary of 15th Divisional Ammunition Column. (Volume 26.) From 1st February 1919. To 28th February 1919.		
War Diary	Quenast	02/02/1919	25/02/1919
Heading	War Diary of 15th Divisional Ammunition Column. (Volume 27.) From 1st March 1919. To 31st March 1919.		
War Diary	Quenast	10/03/1919	26/03/1919
War Diary	Quenast	24/03/1919	24/03/1919
War Diary	Quenast	29/03/1919	31/03/1919
Heading	War Diary of 15th Divisional Ammunition Column (Volume 28) From 1st April 1919. To 30th April 1919.		
War Diary	Quenast	08/04/1919	28/04/1919
War Diary	Quenast	03/05/1919	30/05/1919

WO95/1924(4)

WO95/1924(4)

15TH DIVISION

15TH DIVL AMMN COLUMN
JLY 1915 - MAY 1919

Confidential.

War Diary

of

15th Divisional Ammtn Column

1st January 1917 - 31st January 1917.

VOLUME   13

[signature]

Major, R.A.

Brigade Major 15th Divisional Artillery.

12/6357

15th Division

70th Brigade Ammunition Column
Vol: I.

4-10-4-4-15

Army Form C. 2118.

78th Bde Amm Col
R 77

WAR DIARY
or
INTELLIGENCE SUMMARY.
(Erase heading not required.)

Instructions regarding War Diaries and Intelligence Summaries are contained in F. S. Regs. Part II. and the Staff Manual respectively. Title pages will be prepared in manuscript.

Place	Date	Hour	Summary of Events and Information	Remarks and references to Appendices
Bulford	1-7-15	5-15 pm	Commenced entraining at Amesbury for Southampton	MMBP
	1-7-15	7-30 pm	Left Southampton	
	8-7-15	7.0 am	Disembarked Havre	
	8-7-15	1.0 pm	Arrived rest camp No 1 Havre	
	8-7-15	9-30 pm	Commenced entraining at Havre	
	9-7-15	8-30 pm	Arrived Embaccy via Rouen Amiens & Aubieus	
	10-7-15	5-30 am	Arrived at Wimereux	
	15-7-15	4-0 "	Left Wimereux marching by road	
	"	5-20 pm	Arrived Campagne via St Omer	
	16-7-15	9 am	Left Campagne marching by road	
	16-7-15	5.0 pm	Arrived Thiembronne	
	17-7-15	9.0 am	Left Thiembronne	
	17-7-15	3.30 pm	Arrived Lokagnon via Aire & Lillers	

MMBP
Capt R.F.A.
Commanding 78th Bde Amm Col.

121/7517

15th Division

15th S.A.C.
Vol I
July to Oct 15

Army Form C. 2118

WAR DIARY

INTELLIGENCE SUMMARY.
(Erase heading not required.)

XV Divisional Ammunition Column

Instructions regarding War Diaries and Intelligence Summaries are contained in F. S. Regs., Part II. and the Staff Manual respectively. Title pages will be prepared in manuscript.

Place	Date	Hour	Summary of Events and Information	Remarks and references to Appendices
Bulford	From 3rd July to 9th July		Embarkation Orders received, Commenced mobilization	
	9th July		Mobilization completed	
	10th July		Column left Bulford and embarked for France	
France	11th & 12th July		Column disembarked at Havre	
	13th July		Column concentrated in the field at Louvaignes (Pas de Calais)	
	14th July		Column reached Lapugnoy from Louvaignes via St. Omer, Aire & Lillers. Bivouacs at Lampagne, Berguette	
	From 14th July to 3rd August		Column at Lapugnoy, performed Field Routine duties, drew ammunition up to establishment & issued ammunition to Brigades as requisitioned. Column left for Hesdigneul 3.8.15	
	From 3rd August to 25th September		Column at Hesdigneul, performed Field Routine duties, supplied heavy fatigue parties daily for 4th Coys R.E.	

Army Form C. 2118

WAR DIARY
or
INTELLIGENCE SUMMARY.
(Erase heading not required.)

Instructions regarding War Diaries and Intelligence Summaries are contained in F. S. Regs., Part II. and the Staff Manual respectively. Title pages will be prepared in manuscript.

Place	Date	Hour	Summary of Events and Information	Remarks and references to Appendices
Noeux	3rd August to 25th September		(Continues) Supplies Fatigue parties. Prepared wagons and animals for fatigue, supplies, ammunition requisitions. Column left for	
Noeux les Mines	25th September to 31st October		Supplies Fatigue parties for XV D.A. as required. Routine duties, supplies, ammunition, supplies as requisitioned. Column left for	Supplies Fatigue and carried out supplies to XV Division at Noeux-les-Mines 25-9-15. Noeux Co. Mines performed relief for 4th Coys. R.E. & XV D.A. and Bomb C. Brigades on Hallicourt on 31/10/15

WAR DIARY or INTELLIGENCE SUMMARY

Army Form C. 2118

Place	Date	Hour	Summary of Events and Information	Remarks and references to Appendices
PONNIER	1915 Oct.		The month under review was very quiet. No infantry attack was made either by the Germans or ourselves. The autumnal weather, with its accompanying heavy morning mists, made shooting impossible until well on in the day; and the day's grew rapidly shorter. Both sides have continued their policy of irritating and damaging the enemy without themselves either engaging or inviting an attack. Patrol encounters have been frequent, and snipers remain active. The German artillery is not plentiful, but causes a good deal of material damage and occasionally losses to personnel. Their most formidable weapon has been a minenwerfer which throws a projectile about 15 inches long and 8" diameter. This is propelled slowly through the air and can be seen clearly. The splintering of the time fuze is usually also audible. The eruption of the fly off is nearly perpendicular, and about two seconds elapse before the explosion, which is very violent. The crater formed is said to be 8' deep and 16' across. The damage done to a trench, if it falls in the vicinity, is considerable, but it has caused few casualties, probably because the flight is visible and because a sensible interval has elapsed between arrival and detonation. These naturally	

Army Form C. 2118

WAR DIARY or INTELLIGENCE SUMMARY

(Erase heading not required.)

Place	Date	Hour	Summary of Events and Information	Remarks and references to Appendices
October POMMIER	Oct.		Cause annoyance to the infantry; and every effort has been made to defeat and silence them.	
	18.10		Windscreens have made the wagon lines muddy and uncomfortable. Much delay has occurred in the issue of bricks and materials necessary to the making of horse standings. These are, however, gradually being constructed, and all the men are being brought under cover.	
			On Oct 18th parties consisting of one subaltern and batman 3 telephonists and 2 detachments consisting of No 1 and 6 N.C.O.'s and gunners were exchanged with the 4th Division. 14th Brigade MAILLY MAILLET	
			A/124 — 88th Battery, ENGLEBELMER	
			B/124 — 29th " do	
			C/124 — 134th " do	
			D/124 — 135th " do	
			The period was 18th October — 4th November and the parties had not returned on October 30th. Here D/124 a German Battery which was invisible from any O.P. was engaged. The Forceive worked smoothly and no difficulty was found in communicating with the aeroplane	Clifnhrum [signature] Cmdg. 124 Bde. Artillery.

15th S.A.C.
Vols: 2, 3.

121.
7834.

Army Form C. 2118.

WAR DIARY
or
INTELLIGENCE SUMMARY.
(Erase heading not required.)

Place	Date	Hour	Summary of Events and Information	Remarks and references to Appendices
	November 1915.		15 Divisional Ammunition Column. On November the 1st the Column was at Hallicourt having reached there from Noeux les Mines on 31-10-15. The Column stayed at Hallicourt till the 11th November. At Hallicourt the Column performed the usual duties in connection with supply of ammunition, & fatigues. On the 10th November 250 mules of Column animals were exchanged for draught horses (heavy & light) belonging to an Indian Division. On November 11th the Column marched to Hesdigneul. At Hesdigneul the Column performed the usual duties in connection with ammunition. IVth Corps fatigues were found daily and a large amount of Divisional fatigues were carried out. The Column was at Hesdigneul until the 15th December.	

Army Form C. 2118.

WAR DIARY
or
INTELLIGENCE SUMMARY.
(Erase heading not required.)

Place	Date	Hour	Summary of Events and Information	Remarks and references to Appendices
	December 1915		15th Divisional Ammunition Column	
			From the 1st to the 16th of December the Column was at Hesdigneul performing the usual duties in connection with Ammunition IV Corps & 15th Divisional Fatigues. On 16th December 2 Sections & Headquarters of the Column marched to Auchel whilst No. 3 Section remained in action with the 72nd Brigade R.F.A. The Section remaining at Hesdigneul performed the usual duties in connection with Ammunition till the 31st December and Fatigues. The work of this Section was done under Trying circumstances owing to weather and movements of camp in Hesdigneul. From the 16th December to the 31st December the main body of the Column was at Auchel. Here the Column were "At Rest" but were employed on Fatigues (15th Divisional), and a large amount of refitting was got though.	

Army Forms A3091 (Foolscap)

Cover for Documents

Nature of Enclosures.

War Diary
15th Div. Amn. Col.
Jany – Dec 1916

Notes, or Letters written.

15-t D.A.C.
=
nst. 4
Jan 16

Army Form C. 2118.

WAR DIARY
or
INTELLIGENCE SUMMARY.

(Erase heading not required.)

XVth Div^l Ammⁿ Col.

Place	Date	Hour	Summary of Events and Information	Remarks and references to Appendices
1916.	January 31st.		On January 1st 1916. No. 1 and 2 Sections and Headquarters at Calone. No. 3 Section at Hesdigneul. The 2 Sections and Headquarters took part in the Divisional Review on 5th 6th and 7th January. Returned to Calone and completing the move in ref. - relieving the No 2 D.A.C. Servage No. 1 Sec. joined the Headquarters at Calone on 11th January. Having carried out Ammunition Supply R.F. Fatigues and made trails at Hesdigneul the No 1 and B.C. R.F. Having unmade in detin offri the 16th December 1915. On January 16th the Column marched to Hesdigneul - The Headquarters remaining at Hesdigneul. From the 16th to 31st January the Column carried out the usual duties of Ammunition Supply IV Corps and R.F. Fatigues but was at Hesdigneul on 1st February 1916.	

Army Form C. 2118.

WAR DIARY
or
~~INTELLIGENCE SUMMARY~~

(Erase heading not required.)

XV Div: Amm. Col.

Place	Date	Hour	Summary of Events and Information	Remarks and references to Appendices
			On the 1st February. 1916 the Column was at Headquarters & remained there throughout the month. The Headquarters were at Labussière. The Column carried out its usual duties in the supply of Ammunition, bombs etc. and 111th Corps' R.E. and other fatigues were done during the month. The Column found 70 men for Trench work nightly from the 23rd of the month. The Column completed its service in the 4th Corps at the end of the month.	

15th L.A.C.
vol 5

Army Form C. 2118.

WAR DIARY
INTELLIGENCE SUMMARY.
(Erase heading not required.)

XV Div: Amm. Col.

Place	Date	Hour	Summary of Events and Information	Remarks and references to Appendices
	March		The Column at Ledyguel. The Column carried out the duties of supply of Ammunition to and performed the usual fatigue duties for XV Division; R.E. & 1st Corps. The establishment of the Column was cut down during the month to supply troops to the XV Divisional Brigades and the 4th Division	

15 D. A e
vol 6

DAG
3 Echelon

I am forwarding the War Diary for 15 DAC for April & May — During the month April there was nothing of importance — During May the 15 DAC was reorganised the BACs of 70 Bride 71 Brigde 72nd Brigade were amalgamated with 15 DAC and the 73rd BAC was broken up the men & horses being absorbed by 15 DAC — The strength of 15 DAC ~~became~~ after reorganisation became 815 total Officers & men and 1010 Animals including attached. The reorganisation began on 22nd May & was completed in a few days — The surplus men & Animals will be evacuated in due course —

2.6.16

Army Form C. 2118.

WAR DIARY
or
INTELLIGENCE SUMMARY.

XV Div. Amm Col

(Erase heading not required.)

Instructions regarding War Diaries and Intelligence Summaries are contained in F. S. Regs., Part II. and the Staff Manual respectively. Title pages will be prepared in manuscript.

Place	Date	Hour	Summary of Events and Information	Remarks and references to Appendices
	April		The Column at Hesdigneul carried out the usual duties of supply of Ammunition & bombs, D.A & R.E. fatigues & tombs. Column left for Lespesses. Remained at Lespesses in reserve until the 29th April when for the first time the Column was split up on returning into action. No. 1 Section to Beuvry. No. 2 & Headquarters to Fouquières & No. 3 to Fontinelles. The supply of ammunition recommenced on the 30 April.	

Army Form C. 2118.

WAR DIARY
or
INTELLIGENCE SUMMARY.

(Erase heading not required.)

W.D. 1st Div Amm Col

Place	Date	Hour	Summary of Events and Information	Remarks and references to Appendices
May 1st			The Column split up — No 1 Section at Beuvry, No 2 & Headquarters at Fouquières & No 3 at Fouquereuil carried out the usual duties of Supply of Ammunition & Bombs. DA. & RE. Fatigues until the 21st May when reorganization took place. The Brigade Amm Cols & the Div Amm Col being absorbed into the Nos 1, 2, & 3 Sections. A.Echelon N1 BAC. & N2 BAC. B. Echelon & DAC. On 31st May the reorganized Column was in action carrying out the usual Supply of Ammunition, Bombs D.A. & R.E.) Fatigues No 3 Section at Beuvry No 1-2 Section & Headquarters at Fouquières. No 4. Section at Fouquereuil.	

June 1916.   15 DAC

The reorganisation of the DAC having been completed before the beginning of June the DAC has been working under the new conditions during the month & everything has worked quite satisfactorily under the new conditions —

Several Officers vide Diary have left DAC & joined batteries — others have joined DAC.

30.6.16

L Rowley Abbot
Comm 15 DAC

1st Div
A Col
Vol 9

WAR DIARY
or
INTELLIGENCE SUMMARY.

JUNE 1916   15 H.D.A.C.

Army Form C. 2118.

Place	Date	Hour	Summary of Events and Information	Remarks and references to Appendices
	2nd		2nd Lieut. H.F. NETSON posted 73rd Bde 18 F.A.	June
	14th		2nd Lieut. S.N. WILLOUGHBY posted 70th Bde 18 F.A.	
			2nd Lieut. C. WEIR. posted 70th Bde 18 F.A.	
			2nd Lieut. C.F.W. LAMBART. joined from 70th Bde 18 F.A.	
			2nd Lieut. W.W. EARLY. joined from 70th Bde 16 F.A.	
	23rd		2nd Lieut. A.M. DAVIDSON posted 1215 French Mortar Battery	

I and II Sections at VERQUIGNEUL.
III Section at BEUVRY.
IV Section at FOUQUIERES.

The Column during the month carried out fatigues D.A. + R.E. also the usual supply of ammunition

CONFIDENTIAL.

War Diary

15ᵗʰ D.A.C.

From 1st to 31st July, 1916.

E.W. Boyce
Major, R.A.
Bde Major, 15th Divnl. Arty.

1st August, 1916.

Original 1st July
Army Form C. 2118.

Vol 1 D

WAR DIARY
INTELLIGENCE SUMMARY.

16 R.A.C.

JULY 1916

Place	Date	Hour	Summary of Events and Information	Remarks and references to Appendices
VERQUIGNEUL	1st		Lieut Col the Hon. W. ROWLEY - appointed TOWN MAJOR - BETHUNE.	A4
do	9th		Captain W.H.B. SAVILE assumes temporary command.	A4
do	11th		2nd Lieut W.W. EARLY posted to 71st Bde B.F.A.	A4
do	12th		Lieut Col. J.F. DUNCAN resumes command.	A4
do	19th		For an act of courage on the 29th June 1916 No 32789 B'r C. Young N°1 Sectn 15 Bac was commended in A's R.O. dated 19th July	A4
do	22/23		The Bac moved as part of the Division at 9.30 pm arrived at WAYRANS	A4
WAYRANS	26th	6.30 am 23/7/16 from WAYRANS 6.am to VACQUERIE-LE-BOUCQ arriving at 4 pm.	A4
VACQUERIE LE BOUCQ	27th		from VACQUERIE-LE-BOUCQ at 9.10am to MELERDLLES arriving at 3 pm	A4
do	"		The following officers joined from base W.O.M. Stewart, 2nd Lt D. Vickers, 2nd Lt J.S. Starling	A4
MELERDLLES	28th		from MELERDLLES at 9 am to BOISBERGUES arriving at 11 am	A4
do	"		W.P.D. Vickers posted to 72nd Bgde.	A4
BOISBERGUES	31st		from BOISBERGUES at 6.20am to BOURDON arriving at 1.30 pm	A4
			W.O.M. Stewart posted to 71st Bgde	A3 Journal A4

15th Divisional Artillery.

15th DIVISIONAL AMMUNITION COLUMN R.F.A.

AUGUST 1 9 1 6

C O N F I D E N T I A L.

WAR DIARY.

of

15th Divisional Amtn Column

From 1st August, 1916   to   31st August, 1916.

VOLUME Number __8__

[signature]

Major, R.A.
Brigade Major R.A., 15th Divisional Artillery.

War Diary.
of
15th DAC
1st to 31 Aug 1916
8 Volume

The A.G.o Office
at Base.

This unit moved into its new area and took over from the 33rd DAC. The supply of Ammunition to the Batteries has been heavy throughout. The forward section under the command of Captain A.E. Reed has with the assistance of personnel and six wagons from the other sections of B Echelon met all demands of the Batteries both in ammunition and horses for taking up wagons to the guns.

B Echelon has supplied wagons to the Corps each day.

The unit has also found wagons for the S.A.A. and Salvage dumps.

J. Taylor Duncan
Lieut Col RFA
Commanding 15 Div. A.C.

15th DIVISIONAL
AMMUNITION COLUMN.
31-8-16
No.
Date.

Army Form C. 2118.

WAR DIARY
or
INTELLIGENCE SUMMARY.

(Erase heading not required.)

15th DAC August 1916

Place	Date	Hour	Summary of Events and Information	Remarks and references to Appendices
BOURDON	1-8-16		Encamped. A driver No 22268. J Weir No III Section although a strong swimmer was drowned about 3·20 pm 31·7·16. Efforts to recover his body proved unavailing.	
BAVEINCOURT	2·8·16	4·0 am	DAB marched to BAVEINCOURT, arriving about 11·0 AM	
LAVIEVILLE	3·8·16	9·0 am	Headquarters, No I, II, and IV Sections marched to new area, at LAVIEVILLE, arriving about noon, relieving 19th D.A.C.	
ALBERT	4·8·16	7·0 am	No III Section moved to E.6, c.7, 3, ALBERT to act as a forward ammunition supply section and took up supply from 19th D.A.C. forward section at mid-day 5·5·16.	
MEZEROLLES	7·7·16		P.R.O. 178 dt. 20·8·16 commends No 8926 Cpl. L. B. F. A. Pegg, and 81758 Saddler J. Patmore for being instrumental in saving the life of 90111 S.S.W. Hayman, who was bathing in the river in serious danger of being drowned.	
LAVIEVILLE	14·8·16	6·0 pm	2nd Lieut. S.M. See joined from R.O. & R.F.A. Base Depot and was posted to No II Section.	
do	19·8·16		Medium T.M. Batteries of 15th Division embodied in returns of D.A.B. in accordance with order G.H.Q.	
do	25·8·16		Officers joined from R.O. & R.F.A. Base 2nd Lieut. W. Gutmann, 2nd Lieut. M. Anderson, 2nd Lieut. E. G. J. S. C. Nepean 2nd Lt. J.M. See, and 2nd Lt. M. J. Westerton of No 2 Section posted to 71 and 70 Brigades R.F.A. respectively	
do	26·8·16		2nd Lt. J.C.L. Lee, Lieut. J.H.E. Knox, and 2nd Lt. R.S. Steele joined from 37 Division	
do	30·8·16		do N.K. Cox and 2nd Lieut T. P. Wilkie joined from 39 Division	
do	1·9·16			

CONFIDENTIAL.

War Diary

of

15th Div. Ammtn Column.

From 1st September, 1916 to 30th September, 1916.

Volume Number 9

[signature]

Major, R.A.
Bde Major 15th Divisional Arty.

Confidential
War Diary
of
15th DAC
From 1st to 30 9/16
Volume 9.

D.A.Q. office
at Base

Reference attached the supply of ammunition was carried out satisfactorily, assistance being given to the Batteries by supplying ammunition direct to the guns and teams were also supplied to the Batteries to assist them. The supply was above the normal particularly between the 12th and 16th September. The system of having one section forward and 3 in reserve worked satisfactorily. Wagons, teams and men were supplied daily to the R.E., Infantry and salvage dumps.

1/10/16.

J. Hyes Duncan. Lieut Col RSA
Commdg. 15th D.A.C

Vol 12

Army Form C. 2118.

WAR DIARY
or
INTELLIGENCE SUMMARY.

(Erase heading not required.) 15th HAC September 1916.

Place	Date	Hour	Summary of Events and Information	Remarks and references to Appendices
Lavieville	3.9.16		Lieut C.W. Harper joined on promotion from ranks of 169th Brigade RFA	
do	10.9.16		2/Lieut J.H. Coles joined from R.H.& R.G.A. Cadet Depot. Captain J. Fairquiere posted to D/72 Brigade	
do	15.9.16		Officers joined Lieut A.B. Jacob, 2/Lt R. Lorimer, 2/Lieut G.R. Skinner, 2nd Lieuts B. O'Driscoll, B. Brocklehurst, J.W. Whitehead, B.L.B. Marshall, P.A. Brown, C.R. McG Williams, A.T. Webb, H.G. Green, C. MacNair.	
do	19.9.16	12.0 pm	No 1. Section took over the ammunition section position from No III, who took No 1 Section place at RAINEVILLE	
do	19.9.16	10.0 a	Headquarters No III and No IV Sections marched to St FRATIEN. No I and II remaining in action attached to 23rd Division.	
do	20/9/16		2nd Lieut R.T. Watkins posted to 70th Brigade RFA	
do	25/9/16		No 90054 Sgt J. Nolan, No 1649 Driver D. Vasey and 1923 Driver W. Kemp No III Section awarded the Military Medal for conspicuous bravery whilst delivering ammunition on the night of the 10/11 August 1916.	
do	23/9/16		Captain G.P. Briggs posted to C/171 Brigade R.F.A.	
do	29/9/16		2nd Lieut S.W. Grant posted to A/70 Brigade R.F.A.	

C O N F I D E N T I A L.

War Diary

of

15! D.A.

1st October, 1916.   to   31st October, 1916.

VOLUME. 10

[signature]

Major R.A.
Brigade Major 15th Divisional Arty.

Confidential
War Diary
of
15th D A C
1 - 31 October, 16
Volume X

Reference attached it has been found owing to the multifarious duties allotted to a D.A.C. that the strength of the personnel is not sufficient to comply with demands from batteries and other calls for men and wagons, now looked upon as the regular routine of the unit. If a reserve of 100 men at least could be left with a D.A.C. it would facilitate matters very much.

31/10/16.

Thys. D. Dunlap
Lieut Col R.S.A.
Commanding 15th D A C

Army Form C. 2118.

WAR DIARY
or
INTELLIGENCE SUMMARY.
(Erase heading not required.)

15-MSAC October 1916

Instructions regarding War Diaries and Intelligence Summaries are contained in F. S. Regs., Part II. and the Staff Manual respectively. Title pages will be prepared in manuscript.

Place	Date	Hour	Summary of Events and Information	Remarks and references to Appendices
ST GRATIEN	2/10		Lieut H.E. McCrae joined from 23rd Division & assumed command of No III section.	
do	3/10		2nd Lieut S. Clarkin posted to 70th Brigade RPA, & 2nd Lieut W.E. MacPheron to RPA from 70 Bde Rpa	
do	4/10		2nd Lieut R.E. Farrington and F.W. Whitehead posted to 71st Brigade RPA.	
do	8/10	1.0 pm	Headquarters, No III & 4 sections marched to BECOURT WOOD and joined No I and II sections	
BECOURT	10/10		2nd Lieut C.R. Skinner posted to 71st Brigade RPA. Lieut Jacob A.G. appointed RTO Light Railways	
do	22/10		Lieut A.G. Jacob posted to 72nd Brigade RPA	
do	14/10		Lieut V.G. Hamilton to hospital sick.	
do	12/10		2nd Lieut Sawtell invalided to England (3.10.16) 2nd Lieut F.H. Coles invalided to England	
do	27/10		Lieut R.S. N. Ford to X IV Corps, 2nd Lieut G. Brockhurst and H. Webb to 73rd Brigade RPA.	
do	24/10		2nd Lieut Macrow to 72nd Brigade RPA	
do	29/10		2nd Lieut H. Green to 72nd Brigade RPA	
			Lieut N.E. Stacy and 2nd Lieut B.G. Kavanagh joined from Fort Rosa Base Depot	

Confidential
War diary
of
15th D.A.C
from 1 – 30-11-16
Volume XI

The Officer i/c
A.G's office at the Base

Reference to Diary ammunition was supplied to wagon lines until the 20th instant. After that date ammunition was supplied by railway to new dump at Wagon Lines. This unit has been instrumental in salvaging many thousands of cartridge cases, and many hundreds of live rounds, 18 pdr. and 4·5".

Field
29-11-16.

J. Hughd Dunlop.
Lieut Col R.A
Commanding 15th D.A.C

CONFIDENTIAL.

War Diary.

of

15th Div Arty Col

From 1st November, 1916 - 30th November, 1916.

VOLUME II

1.11.16.

[signature] Captain,

for Bde Major 15th Divisional Arty.

Army Form C. 2118.

WAR DIARY
or
INTELLIGENCE SUMMARY.
(Erase heading not required.)

15 A AC November 1916

Place	Date	Hour	Summary of Events and Information	Remarks and references to Appendices
BECOURT	7/16		2nd Lieuts N.S. Dewey and J. Barker joined from Base	
do	7/16		do L.L.Coran & D.V.Jomin completed MEDIUM T.M. Course & were specially recommended.	
do	12/16		do C.W.Harper invalided to England. 2nd Lieut J.B.P. Lee invalided to England 11.11.16	
do	15/16		do J.O. Sampson and a.D.G.D. Gregory joined from Base.	
do	16/16		do J. Barker admitted to Hospital.	
do	20/16		do L.L. Coran do do	
do	19/16		do A.S. Dew is invalided to England	
do	27/16 10.0 a.m.		90 Section A & L thillon moved to LAVIEVILLE	

CONFIDENTIAL

WAR DIARY

of

15th D.A. Column.

From 1st December, 1916 to 31st December, 1916.

VOLUME IV

[signature] Major, R.A.
Brigade Major 15th Divisional Artillery.

Confidential
War Diary
of
15th D.A.C
From 1st to 31 12/16
Volume 12

To A/Q office at Base

The supply of ammunition being now carried out by railway the greater part of this unit moved back and are now building standings and shelter for the animals.

I am still of the opinion that owing to the demands made upon A.D.A.C. the strength of men should be increased

Field
31/12/16.

J. Fitzpatrick Lieut Col R.A
Commanding 15th D.A.C

Army Form C. 2118.

Vol 15
15th MAC december 1916

WAR DIARY
or
INTELLIGENCE SUMMARY.

(Erase heading not required.)

Place	Date	Hour	Summary of Events and Information	Remarks and references to Appendices
BECOURT	2/12	10 am	No 2 Section moved to LAVIEVILLE	
BECOURT	1/12	10 am	No 3 Section moved to LAVIEVILLE	
BECOURT	12/12	10 am	HQ & No 4 Section moved to LAVIEVILLE	
LAVIEVILLE	15/12	2.30 pm	The unit was inspected by the DRA 15th Division	

WAR DIARY
or
INTELLIGENCE SUMMARY.
(Erase heading not required.)

1st RAC January 1917 Vol 16

Place	Date	Hour	Summary of Events and Information	Remarks and references to Appendices
Lowestoft	3/1/17		Capt H.E. Williams proceeded to England	A
do	10/1/17		Lieut John English in hospital. J. Mackinlay & John Rodent & Lieut Frumley 2nd Lt Gurnam to attachment 2nd Lt Lazarus	A
do	11/1/17		Lieut Frumley 2nd Lt Gurnam on attachment. Posted H.Brig and Capt H. Rhoemder to attachment. 2nd Lt Asmuth to 7th Brigade R.F.A. Lieut Mackinlay 2nd Lt Gurnam to Brigade R.F.A. 2/Lt 1st NZ Rodent to attachment	A
do	20/1/17		2nd Lt Ellis & Bryanpur, 2nd Lt 2 Iohn Gunam, 2/Lt Stinkeer & attached to 7th Brigade R.F.A.	A
do	20/1/17		T.H.Emmer 2nd Lt NZ Borland, 2nd Lt Romance, 2nd Lt NZ Gunn, 2nd Lt King 2/Lt W Lawrence 2/Lt King 2/Lt A. MacGregor 2/Lt A.Mackie & J.T.Hurran 2nd Lt MacGill & Lyons	A
do			Posted to Brigade 2nd Lt NZ Borland H. Gray & 2/Lt Brgde RFA 2/Lt J.R.Martin, A.S.MacGregor, G.Archer to 11th Brge R.F.A. 2/Lt. F Lawrence & 2/Lt J. Gunn to 12th Brigade R.F.A.	A
do	22/1/17		2/Lt Ellis to ambulance hospital (pulmonary)	A
do	24/1/17		Gun Lt Ellis was invalided to England (D.A.H.)	A
do			B.Q.M.S. Prichard B.Q.M.S. Wilkens Wallace hay has been in hospital	A
do	31/1/17		Commum proceed to England on leave G.B.T 2 Blass tapping trenches at 95%	A

Confidential
War Diary
of
15th D.A.C.
From 1st Jany 1917
To 31 do 1917
Volume I

To D.A.G. Base

During the month of January the whole of the 15th D.A.C. remained at rest quarters at LAVIEVILLE. and the supply of ammunition to the two Artillery Brigades of the Divisions in the line was carried out almost entirely by light railway and the D.A.C. was not called on to assist.

Fatigues however were heavy and I would again point out that the system of taking away large parties of men more or less permanently from a mounted unit unaccompanied by their animals or harness operates very adversely against the general efficiency of the unit.

The proportion of men to animals has this month dropped very low on account of these fatigues and animals have undoubtedly suffered.

If these outside duties are to be performed it is imperative that surplus personnel should be allotted to the D.A.C.

(11) The reorganization carried out this month does not call for any comment as it is merely an adjustment of the D.A.C. to conform to the altered constitution of the Divisional Artillery.

Field
31/1/17.

Head
Captain R.F.A.
Commanding 15th D.A.C.

CONFIDENTIAL

WAR DIARY

OF

15th. DIVISIONAL AMMUNITION COLUMN

For month of February 1917.

VOLUME XX

E. Boyce, Maj. R.A.

Brig: General.

Commanding 15th. Divisional Artillery.

War Diary
15th DAC
1st to 28th Feb, 17
Volume II

D.A.C. Base.
With reference to accompanying Diary for February 1917, I have to call attention again to the necessity of increasing the personnel owing to the many calls upon the unit. This month I have had to find 35 men for T M Batteries
33 men for Heavy T M Battery
digging parties in forward and back areas. Apart from this the work of the unit has proceeded. The substitution of mules for horses has increased the efficiency of the work done

Field
28/2/17

J. Tright Duncan Lieut Col R.A
Commanding 15th DAC

Army Form C. 2118.

WAR DIARY
or
INTELLIGENCE SUMMARY.
(Erase heading not required.)

15th A.A.C.   February 1917

Place	Date	Hour	Summary of Events and Information	Remarks and references to Appendices
LAVIEVILLE	29-1-17		2nd Lieut T.H.E. ROWE invalided to England. 'Pulmonary'	out
LAVIEVILLE	1-2-17		2nd Lieut W.E. MacPherson rejoined from Leave England.	in
do	8-2-17	9 am	D.A.C. marched to ST. GRATIEN via LA HOUSSOYE - FRECHENCOURT.	
ST.GRATIEN	9-2-17		Lieut Colonel Fergus Duncan rejoined from Leave England.	in
do	16-2-17	9 am	D.A.C. marched to HEM, via MOLLIENS-AU-BOIS - VILLERS-BOCAGE - TALMAS - BEAUVAL - GEZAINCOURT	
HEM	17-2-17	9 am	D.A.C. marched to CONCHY-SUR-CANCHY via MEZEROLLES - FROHEN-LE-GRAND - VILLER-L'HOPITAL-FORTEL-VACQUERIE BOQ 14	
CONCHY	18-2-17	11-15 am	D.A.C. marched to ST. MICHEL via HAUTE-COTE - ECOIVRES - PT-HOUVIN-HERMIN-LE-SEC - ST.POL	
LAVIEVILLE	18-2-17		2 Lieut L Woods joined from 71 Brigade R.F.A.	in
ST MICHEL	20-2-17		2 Lieut L Woods assumed the duties of TOWN MAJOR RŒLLECOURT - GRANDCAMP-ST MICHEL	out
ST.GRATIEN	13-2-17		Lieut R.T. Wood joined from Base with 120 Reinforcements, & was admitted to Hospital. Convenering.	in

CONFIDENTIAL

War Diary

of

15th D.A.C.

From 1st March 1917 — To 31st March 1917

Volume XV

15 D.A. for A/Q at Base

Reference attached War Diary for March I have to again call attention to the necessity of increasing the establishment of this unit.

It might be possible to find sufficient to find drafts for the Batteries but it is impossible on the present establishment to find drafts for both the Batteries and T.M.B's (Brigade and Heavy)

In addition to drafts since the addition of the B.A.C's this unit is continually called upon for assistance to the Batteries and drafts and personnel have to be maintained

So many men being taken away means that the unit is usually under strength the result being that the luminaries do not get the attention they ought to have and extra work is put on the men remaining. The personnel should in my opinion be increased by at least 10 % Officers & men.

31/3/17.

J. Thynne Dutton
Lt Col RFA
Commandt 15 D.A.C.

WAR DIARY
or
INTELLIGENCE SUMMARY. 15th D.A.C. MARCH.

Army Form C. 2118.

Vol 58

Place	Date	Hour	Summary of Events and Information	Remarks and references to Appendices
ST. MICHEL	6-3-17		Lieut R.T. Wood posted to 71st Brigade R.F.A., 2nd Lieut M.G. Liddle admitted to Hospital (PLEURISY)	OR
do	8-3-17		2nd Lieut W.W. Gunby posted to W16 Heavy T.M.B., Column moved to HABARCQ, via MAIN ARRAS ROAD – HERMAVILLE –	OR
HABARCQ	12-3-17		do W.G. Woods, rejoined from hospital.	OR
do	13-3-17		Captain A.R. Rawson, admitted to Hospital.	OR
do	14-3-17		Lieut V.B. Hamilton admitted to Hospital. (rejoined 18-3-17)	OR
do	15-3-17		Lieut H. Eaton-Shaw, posted to Army Field Artillery 72 Brigade R.F.A.	OR
do	16-3-17		2nd Lieut Edwards rejoined from Swan, Major St Michel, 2nd Lts W.B. Harrison & S.A. Morton joined from Base	OR
do	21-3-17		Lieut V.C. Hamilton proceeded on leave to U.K. (urgent private affairs)	OR
do	24-3-17		Captain H. McC. Williams joined from Base	OR
do	25-3-17		Captain H. McC. Williams posted to 70th Brigade R.F.A., 2nd Lieut S.A. Morton posted to 71st Brigade R.F.A.	OR
do	27-3-17		Column moved to DUISANS via AGNEZ-LE-DUISANS.	OR
DUISANS	29-3-17		2nd Lieut S. Lemond to 70th Brigade R.F.A.	OR

CONFIDENTIAL.

War Diary

of

15^t D. A. C.

VOLUME 2

From 1st April 1917 . 30th April, 1917.

Army Form C. 2118.

WAR DIARY
or
INTELLIGENCE SUMMARY. April 1917

(Erase heading not required.)

Place	Date	Hour	Summary of Events and Information	Remarks and references to Appendices
DUISANS	31.3.17		2nd Lieut C Kehoe joined on Commission from 1st Reserve	al
do	4.4.17		do W C Kehoe posted to 70th Brigade R.F.A.	al
do	6.4.17		do V C Hamilton reported from leave to England	al
do	8.4.17		2nd Lieuts L W Toomer L Westwood, and S G Stones joined from Base	al
do	9.4.17		No 2 Section detached temporarily with 71st Brigade R.F.A.	al
do	10.4.17		Headquarters No I and 3 Sections moved by road to ARRAS.	al
ARRAS	11.4.17		No 2 Section rejoined the Column.	al
do	16.4.17		2nd Lieut S G Stones posted to 70th Brigade R.F.A. 2nd Lieut L Westwood to 71st Brigade R.F.A.	al
do	20.4.17		2nd Lieut W A Slade, G P Woolland 40? Bateman joined from Base.	al
do	21.4.17		2nd Lieut W.O. Slade to 70th Brigade R.F.A. 2nd Lieut W H Bateman to 71st Brigade R.F.A.	al
do	23.4.17		72161 Sergt A T Shepard, 79321 Cpl Clarke, & 77904 Gr Blunn awarded Military Medal	al

War diary of 15th DAC from 1-4-17 to 30/4/17 volume 4.

The A.G's Office at Base

Reference attached the work done by this unit has been arduous and the lack of personnel has at times been severely felt. I have drawn attention before to the fact that in my opinion the personnel should be increased by 10% of establishment

If re-inforcements for Batteries are to be supplied and labour found for the work which a D.A.C has now to undertake the 10% increase should be with the D.A.C so that no hiatus should occur between the sending of personnel to Batteries and the arrival of a draft from the Base

Field
1-5-17

J. Thynne Duncan Lieut Col R.A
Commanding 15th D.A.C

CONFIDENTIAL.

WAR DIARY

of

15th DIVISIONAL AMMUNITION COLUMN.

from 1st May, 1917.   to 31st May, 1917.

(Volume 5).

War Diary
of
15th D.A.C
for May 1917
Volume 5.

The A.G's Office
at Base

Reference attached the establishment should be increased by at least 10% in gunners. During the operations the last two months assistance had to be obtained from other units to carry on the work. This was due partly to the shortage of personnel but even if I had been at full strength I should not have been able to carry on the necessary work without assistance

Field.
31/5/17

J. ??? Duncan
Lieut Colonel R.A
Commanding 15th D.A.C.

Army Form C. 2118.

WAR DIARY
or
INTELLIGENCE SUMMARY.

(Erase heading not required.)

May 1917.

Place	Date	Hour	Summary of Events and Information	Remarks and references to Appendices
ARRAS	9.5.17		Officers joined from Base, 2nd Lieuts R. Lutter Pratt, J.C. Ogilvie, C.E. Hughes-Davies.	
do	17.5.17		do do do 2nd Lieuts J.C. Peirce, A Hayward, J Sandeman, I.J. Irwin	
do	20.5.17		do do do 2nd Lieut J.J.N. de Pencier.	
do	24.5.17	7.30 a	D.A.C. marched from ARRAS to HABARCQ	
HABARCQ	25.5.17	10 am	D.A.C. marched from HABARCQ to ETREE-WAMIN	
ETREE-WAMIN	26.5.17	4 pm	D.A.C. marched from ETREE-WAMIN to AMBROMETZ (NEW BILLETING AREA)	
AMBROMETZ	29.5.17		2nd Lieut A LAMOND joined from Base	

CONFIDENTIAL.

WAR DIARY

of

15th DIVISIONAL AMMUNITION COLUMN

From 1st June, 1917. To 30th June 1917.

VOLUME 6.

War Diary
of
15th D A C
1st to 30/6/17
Volume 6.

To A.G's Office at Base

Reference attached I can only reiterate my former remarks in previous months viz that the personnel of gunners in a Divisional Ammunition Column should be increased. Men have to be sent on special courses such as signalling, gunnery and trench mortars, which means that the unit is generally short in numbers for work to be done

I consider that the establishment in gunners of each section should be 70 to enable the unit to comply with the demands made upon it.

Lieut. Colonel R.F.A.
COMMANDING 15. D. A. C.

Army Form C. 2118.

WAR DIARY
or
INTELLIGENCE SUMMARY.
(Erase heading not required.)

June 1917

Instructions regarding War Diaries and Intelligence Summaries are contained in F. S. Regs., Part II. and the Staff Manual respectively. Title pages will be prepared in manuscript.

Place	Date	Hour	Summary of Events and Information	Remarks and references to Appendices
AUBROMETZ	7-6-17	am	2nd Lieut A.J. MacTavish joined from R.H. & R.F.A. Base Depot.	alf
do	16-6-17	5·30 am	D.A.C. marched to BERGUENEUSE. via. CROISETTE - PIERREMONT - FLEURY.	alf
BERGUENEUSE	17-6-17	6·25 a.m.	D.A.C. marched to ST HILAIRE via FONTAINE-LEZ-BOULANS - YVESTREHEM.	alf
ST HILAIRE	18-6-17	5·40 A.M.	D.A.C. marched to STEENBECQUE, VIA. LAMBRES - NEUPRE - PECQUER - BOESEGHEM.	alf
STEENBECQUE	20-6-17	5·42 AM	D.A.C. marched to EECKE ARTILLERY AREA VIA MORBECQUE - HAZEBROUCK - SYLVESTRECAPPEL.	alf
EECKE A.A.	26-6-17	10·15 p.m.	D.A.C marched to WATOU ARTILLERY AREA, VIA STEENVOORDE.	alf
WATOU	26-6-17	7·0 p.m.	No 3 Section "B" Echelon D.A.C. marched to FORWARD AREA	alf
WATOU	27-6-17	6·0 p.m.	No 1 Section. D.A.C. sent up R.A. wagons to FORWARD AREA.	alf
WATOU	28-6-17		2nd Lieut B.G. Kavanagh admitted to Hospital (Sick)	alf
WATOU	29-6-17	8·0 a.m	Headquarters D.A.C. marched to forward area.	alf

CONFIDENTIAL.

WAR DIARY

of

15th Divisional Ammunition Column

(Volume 7)

From 1st July 1917.

To 31st July 1917.

WAR DIARY or INTELLIGENCE SUMMARY.

(Erase heading not required.)

Army Form C. 2118.

July 1917

Place	Date	Hour	Summary of Events and Information	Remarks and references to Appendices
BRANDHOEK	1/7/17		2nd Lieut L.C. Pierce posted to V.15 Trench Mortar Battery	A
do	5/7/17		2nd Lieut R. Sutton Pratt posted to 70th Brigade B.T.M.	A
do	7/7/17		2nd Lieut C.E. Hughes Davis posted to 71st Brigade B.T.M., 2nd Lieut A. Hayward to Army Rest Camp	A
do	10/7/17		No 3 section B Echelon moved back to WATOU ARTILLERY AREA	
do	13/7/17		2nd Lieut J. Sandeman posted to Z.15 T.M. Battery	A
do	16/7/17		2nd Lieut H. Mac Tavish attended a course of Heavy Trench Mortars at 2nd Army School till 30th inst	A
do	17/7/17		2nd Lieut J.J. Quin attended a course of 6" Trench Mortars at 2nd Army School till 21st inst	A
do	20/7/17		No 11120 Sergeant John Gardner and 78351 Driver Frederick James Brook awarded Military Medal	A
do	26/7/17		No 16218 Sergeant William Reacon awarded Military Medal	A
do	29/7/17		No 3 Section B Echelon rejoined at BRANDHOEK.	A
do	29/7/17		2nd Lieut A Hayward admitted to Maj Statismon Hospital sick.	A
			908501 Driver Ray Herbert awarded Military Medal.	A

CONFIDENTIAL.

WAR DIARY

of

15th Divisional Ammunition Column

From 1st August 1917.   To 31st August 1917.

(Volume 8).

War Diary
of
15th DAC
from 1st to 31st 7/17
Volume 7

The A/Q Office
at Base

This unit has had many demands made upon it for fatigues such as digging parties for Batteries, & the manning of ammunition dumps, also men have been taken away for courses. The establishment of gunners is not sufficient to meet the demands made necessitating the employment of drivers to the detriment of animals and harness. In my opinion the establishment of gunners should be raised by 50%

Lieut. Colonel R.F.A.
COMMANDING 15, D.A.C.

War Diary
of
15th DAC
for August 17
Volume 8.

D.A.G's Office
at Base

The supply of ammunition has been abnormal. The ability to meet the demand for labour on dumps is unduly affected by the small establishment of gunners. The establishment of gunners should be increased by 50%

Field
31/8/17

J Tryh Duncan Lieut Col R.a
Commdg 15th DAC

WAR DIARY
or
INTELLIGENCE SUMMARY.
(Erase heading not required.)

Army Form C. 2118.

August 1917   Vol 23

Place	Date	Hour	Summary of Events and Information	Remarks and references to Appendices
BRAND HOEK	3-8-17		2nd Lieut. J.J. Elliott, R.A. Nugent, W.J.H. Macdonald, W.J.R. Bedford from N.Z.A.R.Q.A Base depot	A
do.	5-8-17		2nd Lieut. O.F.W. Lambert to 55th BAC, 2nd Lieut. P.P. Boran, J.A. Elliott, & W.R. Bedford to 71st Howitzer R.A; 2nd Lieut. H.J. Mac Tavish, R.A. Nugent & W.J. Macdonald to 70th Brigade R.A.	A
do	31-7-17		2nd Lieut. R.J. Kavanagh to England (sick)	A
do	7-8-17		2nd Lieut. R.S. Steele to Hospital Sick	A
do	21-8-17		2nd Lieuts. R.P. Chivers, J.E. Stephens, & A. Martin from Base, 2nd Lieut. R.P. Chivers & J. Stephens to 70th Brigade R.A.	A
do	23-8-17		2nd Lieut. R.S. Maguire from Base depot.	A
do	25-8-17		No. 157940 Sgt. J. Russell awarded military medal for gallantry in the field	A
do	27-8-17		2nd Lieut. J.J. Hardman, R.W. Robertson & W. Strachan from Base depot.	A
do	29-8-17	11.0am	S.A.C. marden to WATOU ARTILLERY AREA.	A
do	3-8-17		2nd Lieuts. H. Hardman & W.H. Strachan to 71st Brigade R.A.	A
do	29-8-17		2nd Lieut. W.E. Macpherson to hospital sick	A
do	31-8-17		Lieut. J.J. Finn to 15th Divisional T. Motor Battery	A

O.F. Cashman

CONFIDENTIAL.

WAR DIARY

of

15th Divisional Ammunition Column

(Volume 9).

From 1/9/17. To 30/9/17.

War Diary
of
15th D.A.C.
from 1-30 9/17
Volume 9

The D.A.C. Base
G.H.Q 3rd Echelon

I am still of the opinion that the personnel of gunners should be increased to meet the demands made upon the unit which are caused owing to exigencies of active service.

Field
1-10-17

J Hugh Duncan Lieut Col RHA
Commanding 15th D.A.C.

Army Form C. 2118.

WAR DIARY
or
INTELLIGENCE SUMMARY.
(Erase heading not required.)

September 1917

Place	Date	Hour	Summary of Events and Information	Remarks and references to Appendices
WATOU	2/9/17	11.20 am	H.q. No 1 Section & 3 of B Echelon moved to NOORDPEENE via BROCKANDT - WEMAERS CAPPEL. No 2 Section & 2/3 B Echelon moved to WORMHOUDT via HOUTKERQUE - HERZEELE.	
CASSEL	4/9/17	10.41	H.q. No 1 Section & 3 B Echelon entrained at CASSEL for ARRAS, thence by road to NOYELLETTE	
ESQUELBECQ	do	various	No 2 Section & 2/3 B Echelon entrained at ESQUELBECQ for ARRAS, and ditto.	
NOYELLETTE	6/9/17	am	Captain G.R.Rawran met with an accident & was admitted to hospital.	
do	7/9/17	9.40 am	DAC marched to ARRAS district via HABARCQ - LORISSET	
ARRAS	14/9/17		2nd Lieut. J. Stack. H. Ogilvie & R.W. Robertson proceeded to III Army Schol of Musketry Course	
do	1/7/17		2nd Lieut. I.W. Woods & W.G. Woods promoted Lieutenants vide Gazette.	
do	20/9/17		2nd Lieuts J. Metcalf, W.A. Atkinson & R.A. Brown joined from Base HAVRE. DAC war re-organized	
do	6/9/17		2nd Lieut S.M.D. Hackett joined from Base HAVRE & was posted to 71st Brigade DAM 20/9/17	
do	1/9/17		2nd Lieut J. Garrard joined on Commission from 6/46 Army 71st Brigade	
1/Aug 31 FLUCHÉ ARRAS	23/9/17		2nd Lieut. W. Trask admitted to hospital whilst undergoing course	
do	24/9/17		2nd Lieut. Metcalf & 71st Brigade DAM, 2 Lieut T.F. Wallace to 10th Bde R.F.A.	
ARRAS	27/9/17		Captain G.R. Rawran rejoined from hospital & posted to 2nd in Command of DAC. Brigadier Captain A. Taylor D.A.A. joined from 71st Bde R.A. Lieut. Forsey Maggs from Base 24/9/17	
ARRAS	28/9/17		2nd Lieut R.A. Maguire posted to 71st Brigade D.A.M. 2nd Lieut H. Ogilvie & R.W. Robertson rejoined from Course. W.R. Watts WAES 29/9/17	

R.W.[signature]

CONFIDENTIAL.

WAR DIARY

of

15th Divisional Ammunition Column

From 1st October 1917.   To 31st October, 1917.

(Volume 10).

War Diary
of
15th DAC
from
1st to 31st Oct 17
Volume X.

To A.G's Office
Base

I have no remarks to
make other than those usually
made by Lt Col Duncan, the
permanent commander of the
unit —

Head
Captain RFA
for Lieut Col RFA
Commanding 15th DAC

Army Form C. 2118.

WAR DIARY
or
INTELLIGENCE SUMMARY.
(Erase heading not required.)

October 1917

Place	Date	Hour	Summary of Events and Information	Remarks and references to Appendices
ARRAS	5/10/17		2nd Lieut H. Frank rejoined from Hospital	
ARRAS	6/10/17		do H. Frank posted to X 15 Trench Mortar Battery	
ARRAS	7/10/17		Lieut V.B Hamilton on leave to U.K. 9- to 23 (Extension of 3 days granted)	
ARRAS	8/10/17		Lieut (/Capt) R. Bateman leave to U.K. 10-20.10.17	
ARRAS	10/10/17		Lieut B.H. Mac Manus performing duties of Div Gas Officer at No Gas School to 29/10/17	
ARRAS	19/10/17		2nd Lieut F.L. Bunn joined from III Army Arty School, & posted to / Brigade RSA 24.10.17	
ARRAS	26/10/17		do Capt Bateman posted to 7 N.Z. Artillery	
ARRAS	27/10/17		do W.S Macpherson rejoined from Base (convalescent)	

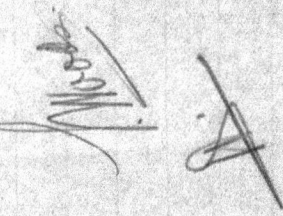

CONFIDENTIAL.

WAR DIARY

of

15th Divisional Ammunition Column

(Volume 11)

From 1st November 1917.   To 30th November 1917.

The A.G's Office
at Base

War Diary
of
15th D.A.C
from 1st to 30th/11/17
VOLUME II

I have nothing to add to the remarks usually made by the permanent Commander of the unit.

Head
Capt RFA
Tempy Comdg 15th DAC

30/11/17

Army Form C. 2118.

WAR DIARY
or
INTELLIGENCE SUMMARY.

(Erase heading not required.)

November 1917.

Place	Date	Hour	Summary of Events and Information	Remarks and references to Appendices
ARRAS	4-11-17		2nd Lieut R.M. BROWN to III Army Arty School course.	
do	6-11-17		Lieut E.H. MacManus struck off.	
do	8-11-17		Captain I. SPIERS Glasgow Yeomanry attached	
do	24-11-17		2nd Lieut N.S. GILMOUR to 71 Brigade R.F.A. 2nd Lieut A. MARTIN to 70th Brigade R.F.A. Lieut J.G. KENNEY and 2nd Lieut A.B. MARTIN joined from 71st Brigade R.F.A.	
do	16-11-17		Lieut Col J Fergus DUNCAN. D.S.O. Leave to United Kingdom.	
do	17-11-17		701 Section detached with IV Corps	

1577 Wt.W10791/1773 500,000 1/15 D.D.&L. A.D.S.S./Forms/C. 2118.

CONFIDENTIAL.

WAR DIARY

of

15th Divisional Ammunition Column.

(Volume 12.)

From 1st December 1917.   To 31st December 1917.

<u>Confidential</u>

War Diary
15th D.A.C.
From 1 - 31.12.17
Volume 12.

The A.G's Office
   at Base

        I would point out that the Establishment of 150 Gunners in this unit is not sufficient to provide drafts for the Brigades and Trench Mortar Batteries, and enable the work of the unit to be carried on. 68 gunners alone have to be trained for Trench Mortar Batteries which leaves 82 gunners for drafts to Batteries and employed men in the unit. If the establishment were increased by 68 gunners the number to be trained for T.M.B's, it would facilitate the work of the unit.

Field
31.12.17.

J Hugh Dunn Lieut Col. R.F.A.
Commanding 15th D.A.C.

WAR DIARY
or
INTELLIGENCE SUMMARY. December 1917

Army Form C. 2118.

Vol 27

Place	Date	Hour	Summary of Events and Information	Remarks and references to Appendices
ARRAS	4th		2nd Lieut. W.E. Macpherson Leave to U.K. Leave extended to 2-1-18 by W.O. on medical grounds	AA
do	9th		Lieut J.J. Finn joined from 16th Trench Mortar Battery	AA
do	13th		2nd Lieut W.A. Colquhoun and W.R.M.C. Potter joined from Base	AA
do	14th		W.H.C. Quinn joined from Base	AA
do	18th		Captain W. Read Leave to U.K. 19-12-17 to 18-1-18, Lieut Lwords leave to U.K. 19-12-17 to 2-1-18	AA
do	21st		No.1 Section rejoined from being attached to II Corps	AA
do			No.1 Section marched to Beaukencourt. 30-11-17 to Bus. 20-11-17, to Metz 21-11-17, to Bus 30-11-17, to Sorrel 10-12-17, to Beaukencourt 20-12-1) to Arras (21-12-17)	
do	24th		2nd Lieut R.M Brown posted to 71st Brigade R.A	AA
do	26th		W.R.M.C. Potter posted to 70 Brigade R.A	AA
do	30th		W.A. Colquhoun to the ___ ___ Veterinary course	AA

CONFIDENTIAL.

WAR DIARY

of

15th Divisional Ammunition Column

(Volume 13)

From 1st January 1918   To 31st January 1918.

Army Form C. 2118.

WAR DIARY
or
INTELLIGENCE SUMMARY.
(Erase heading not required.)

Original
January 1918 Vol 28

Place	Date	Hour	Summary of Events and Information	Remarks and references to Appendices
ARRAS	3.1.18		Lieut F.J.Finn leave U.K. 3 – 17.1.18	W.O.
do	5.1.18		2nd Lieut W.H.C.Quinn. Musketry Course Warley 5 – 27.1.18	W.O.
do	12.1.18		do to a Co'ynhun completed Veterinary Course 12.1.18	W.O.
do	13.1.18		do W.E. MacPherson struck off.	W.O.
do	25.1.18		Captain A. Taylor leave to U.K. 25.1.18 – 8.2.18	W.O.
do	25.1.18		Captain W. Read, Lieut W.G. Worth proceeded to ROUEN for Indian Course	W.O.
do	25.1.18		Captain A. Flatman leave to U.K. 25.1.18 – 11.2.18	W.O.

CONFIDENTIAL.

WAR DIARY

of

15th Divisional Ammunition Column

Volume 14.

From 1st February 1918.   To 1st March 1918.

WAR DIARY or INTELLIGENCE SUMMARY

Army Form C. 2118.

February 1918

Place	Date	Hour	Summary of Events and Information	Remarks and references to Appendices
ARRAS	1.2.18		2nd Lieuts A. Stanway, G.W. Shepherd, A.M. Wynhart, & A.B. Platt joined from III Army School	
do	9.2.18		2nd Lieut R.J. Murtoo joined from Base. Lieut J.J. Finn posted to 5th T.M. Brigade	
do	10.2.18		Lieut V.C. Hamilton posted to 70th Brigade R.S.A.	
do	13.2.18		2nd Lieut A.P. Burgon Shove joined from Base	
do	14.2.18		2nd Lieut R.J. Bleveleau & R.J. Thompson joined from Base	
do	11.2.18		2nd Lieut A.M. Wynhart posted to 15 T.M. Brigade. Lieuts Brook Bulkeley & Nabarr posted to 70th & 71st Battalion respectively	
do	16.2.18		2nd Lieut J.B. Aspinall joined from Base	
do	19.2.18		2nd Lieut J.B. Aspinall and R.K. Thompson posted to 70th and 71st Bde respectively. Lieut J.G. Kenney to 7th Field Ambulance sick. Captain W. Flatman rejoined from internment of leave Auty W.O.	
do	18.2.18		Lieut W.G. Woods rejoined from Indian Cavalry advanced Base	
do	21.2.18		2nd Lieut A.R. Field and B.C. Ogle joined from Base	
do	23.2.18		A.R. Field posted to 15th T.M. Brigade	
do			Captain R.R. Wilson proceeded on leave 11-25th. 2nd Lieut Gannon 19th-3rd. Lieut W. Woods from 21.2.18 - 7.3.18.	

15th Divisional Artillery.

15th DIVISIONAL AMMUNITION COLUMN R.F.A.

MARCH 1918

CONFIDENTIAL.

WAR DIARY

of

15th Divisional Ammunition Column
(Volume 15)

From 1st March 1918.   to 31st March 1918.

WAR DIARY
or
INTELLIGENCE SUMMARY.
(Erase heading not required.)

Army Form C. 2118.

March 1918   J.W. 30

Place	Date	Hour	Summary of Events and Information	Remarks and references to Appendices
ARRAS	1-7th		Lt Col Fergusson, Duncan and 2nd Lieut A B Martin proceeded on leave to U.K.	
do	2nd 3/18		2nd Lieut Rutherford posted to 70th Brigade Road. 2nd Lieut W R Betz who came from XVII Corps Cyclists.	
do	4th		Lieut V G Hamilton from 70 Bde & Lieut 99 Bn from 15th Trench Mortars, 2nd Lieut H Munro to 15 R.I. Res.	
do	4th		2nd Lieuts W J. Quinn, J Wilkie & H Foster to 70 Bde RGA. 2nd Lieuts R Munro & Cooper to 71st Brigade RGA	
do	7th		Lieut A.G. Woods reported from leave	
do	15th		Lt Col J.M. Duncan D.S.O. and 2nd Lieut A.B. Martin reported from leave	
do	22nd		Headquarters & Section marched to ACHICOURT and took the place of 4th Div AC ROUTE	
			ARRAS - ST POL ROAD - WAGONLIEU - DAINVILLE - ACHICOURT	
do	27th		Headquarters & Section marched to DAINVILLEWOOD	
do	28th		Headquarters & Section marched to DUISANS via WAGONLIEU	
do	29th		2nd Lieut A.G. Park and J.E. Mann posted to 70 th Brigade R.G.A.	

15th Divisional Artillery

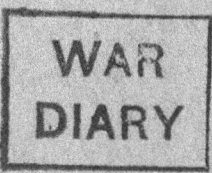

15th DIVISIONAL AMMUNITION COLUMN

APRIL 1918

CONFIDENTIAL.

WAR DIARY

of

15th Divisional Ammunition Column.

(Volume 16).

From 1st April 1918.   To 30th April 1918.

Army Form C. 2118.

WAR DIARY
or
INTELLIGENCE SUMMARY.
(Erase heading not required.)

April 1918

Vol 31

Place	Date	Hour	Summary of Events and Information	Remarks and references to Appendices
DUISANS	3-4-18		Capt Geo. O. Clough, 2nd Lieut C. Beatty joined from Base.	appx
do	6-4-18		Headquarters No 1 and 3 Sections moved from DUISANS to HABARCQ via AGNEZ-LES-DUISANS.	appx
HABARCQ	4-4-18		Headquarters No 1 and 3 Section moved to MONTENESCOURT.	appx
do	7-4-18		Lieut E. Jefferson, 2nd Lieut J. Ralson & J.W. Leader joined from Base	appx
Montenescourt	19-4-18		2nd Lieut V.E. Beatty to 71st Brigade RFA. 2nd Lieut R.J. Bleeden attached to No 96 A.A. Battery.	appx
Habarcq	9-4-18		Capt J.F.D. Clough Invalided to England	appx
Montenescourt	24-4-18		No 3 Section moved to MARLES-LES-MINES with Infantry. No 2 Section joined column at MONTENESCOURT.	appx

1577 Wt. W10791/1773 500,000 1/15 D.D. & L. A.D.S.S./Forms/C. 2118.

CONFIDENTIAL.

WAR DIARY

of

15th Divisional Ammunition Column.

(Volume 17.)

From 1st May 1918.

To 31st May 1918.

Army Form C. 2118.

WAR DIARY
or
INTELLIGENCE SUMMARY.
(Erase heading not required.)

15th J.A.C. May 1918.

No 32

Place	Date	Hour	Summary of Events and Information	Remarks and references to Appendices
Montenescourt	1.5.18		2nd Lieut F.J. Higham joined from Base.	
	4.5.18		Headquarters and No 1 and 2 Sections moved from MONTENESCOURT to ANZIN via GOUVES - DUISANS - ETRUN.	
			S.A.A. Section marched to MONTENESCOURT from MARLES-LES-MINES	
ANZIN	9.5.18		Headquarters and No 1 and 2 Sections marching to MARŒUIL and BRAY	
	10.5.18		Sent By Motor Lorries to Gonaville. Struck off the Strength.	
			Lieut L.C. Marie joined from Base	
MARŒUIL	18.5.18		S.A.A. Section marched to AGNEZ-LES-DUISANS	
	19.5.18			
	21.5.18		Lieut Col. A. Rogers Duncan - mentioned in dispatches	
			No. 43404 Cpl M. Perry M.O. D.C.M. mentioned in dispatches	
			Captain J. Flatman (Stepland) awarded to No. 7 C.C.S. Sick.	
	24.5.18		Lieut F.L.G. Fox joined from Base and was posted to 71st Brigade R.F.A.	
	25.5.18		Lieut L.M. Brown's SANIC (attached) posted to 115 French Motor Park.	
	28.5.18		Lieut L.C. Price posted to 74th Div. Artillery.	

CONFIDENTIAL.

WAR DIARY

OF

15th Divisional Ammunition Column.

(volume 18)

From 1st June 1918.   To 30th June 1918.

Army Form C. 2118.

WAR DIARY
or
INTELLIGENCE SUMMARY.
(Erase heading not required.)

15th D.A.C. June 1918

Vol 33

Place	Date	Hour	Summary of Events and Information	Remarks and references to Appendices
MARDEUIL	6.6.18		Lieut J.J. Finn posted to 71st Brigade R.F.A.	
	7.6.18		2nd Lieut L.F. Rowell joined from 71st Brigade R.F.A.	
	8.6.18		2nd Lieut R.F. Cleveland posted to "B" Anti Aircraft Battery	
	13.6.18		Chaplain A. Tatman. Voluntarily transferred to England 31/5/18, struck off strength.	
			Lieut E. Jefferson posted to 70th Brigade R.F.A.	
			Lieut L. Woods rejoined from 15th D.A.H.Q. and appointed adjutant with effect from 31.5.18 vice Major A. Tatman.	
	15.6.18		2nd Lieut J.R. Blackley joined from Base	
	18.6.18		Lieut J.M. Bonner joined from Base. Proceeded to join 71st Brigade R.F.A. 19.6.18	
	20.6.18		2nd Lieut J.R. Blackley posted to 70th Brigade R.F.A.	
	22.6.18		Headquarters, and Nos 1 and 2 Sections marched to GOUVES nr DUISANS	
	23.6.18		Captain. H. Lear rejoined from Indian R.A. A.B.D. ROUEN	
			151 Indian Jemmile John (Capt in Lieut &c.) from ROUEN.	
			6080 T.R.Sm Chatfield E. and 51479 B.Sm. Hodge S. awarded "Meritorious Service Medal" in H.M. Kings Birthday Honours.	

CONFIDENTIAL.

WAR DIARY

of

15th Divisional Ammunition Column.

(Volume 19)

From 1st July 1918.   To 31st July 1918.

Army Form C. 2118.

WAR DIARY
or
INTELLIGENCE SUMMARY.
(Erase heading not required.)

15th D.A.C.   July 1918.   Vol 34

Place	Date	Hour	Summary of Events and Information	Remarks and references to Appendices
GOUVES	1.7.18		LIEUT V.C.HAMILTON admitted to hospital - sick. 2ND LIEUT. W.A.COLQUHOUN rejoined	
	11.7.18		from XVII Corps Infantry School, Signalling Course.	
	15.7.18		CAPT. L. WOODS. Leave to PARIS PLAGE - 5 days.	
			Column marched to FREVIN CAPELLE. H.Q, Nos 1 + 2 Sections from GOUVES. SAA Section	
FREVIN-CAPELLE	16.7.18		from AGNEZ LES DUISANS.	
			Column moved to SACY-LE GRAND (Department of OISE). March route to TINQUES. Entrained	
			at TINQUES, on night of 16/17.7. proceeded via AMIENS & BEAUVAIS to LAIGNEVILLE. Detrained at	
			LAIGNEVILLE on night of 17/18.5. continued by march route to SACY-LE GRAND.	
			Bombed by E.A. whilst entraining at TINQUES. No casualties to personnel.	
SACY LE GRAND	19.7.18		Column marched to VERBERIE, via PONT-ST-MAXENCE.	
VERBERIE	20.7.18		Column marched to VIEUX MOULIN.	
VIEUX MOULIN	21.7.18		Column marched to RETHEUIL.	
RETHEUIL	22.7.18		Column marched to SOUCY.	
	17.7.18		2nd Lieut W.A.Colquhoun. Leave to U.K.	
	30.7.18		2nd Lieut A.Hathaway. Leave to U.K.	

[signature]

C O N F I D E N T I A L.

W A R   D I A R Y

of

15th Divisional Ammunition Column.

From 1st August 1918.   To 31st August 1918.

(volume 20).

Army Form C. 2118.

WAR DIARY
or
INTELLIGENCE SUMMARY.
(Erase heading not required.)

15th D.I.G.   August 1918.

Vol 35

Place	Date	Hour	Summary of Events and Information	Remarks and references to Appendices
Soucy	1.8.18		Captain A. Woods Leave to U.K. 2nd Lieut W.H. Colquhoun rejoined from leave 29/8.	W/C
	4.8.18		Column marched to CHANIANT par SENLIS (OISE) via CREPY.	W/C
CHANIANT	5.8.18		Marched to SARRON via PONT ST MAXENCE.	W/C
SARRON	6.8.18		Marched with affiliated Brigades to LAIGNEVILLE, LIANCOURT, PONT ST MAXENCE & CLERMONT for entraining. Proceeded to FREVENT & TINCQUES via AMIENS.	W/C
	6/7/8/18		Detrained. Marched to MAGNICOURT SUR CANCHE.	W/C
MAGNICOURT	9.8.18		Following Officers joined, Capt W.M. Haddock, Lieut G.B. Page, 2nd Lieut G.W. Mitchell, Lt R. Baylton & 150 W/C	W/C
	10.8.18		No 514279 B.S.M. Hodge a. and 143401 B.S.M Berry M.B. DCM awarded CROIX de GUERRE.	W/C
	10.8.18		2nd Lieut J.H. Hardman joined. 11-8-18 2nd Lieut J. Baldwin to hospital sick.	W/C
	17.8.18		Column marched to MONTENESCOURT area. 2nd Lieut E.J. Duncan joined.	W/C
MONTENES- COURT	20.8.18		Lieut J.H. Hardman leave to U.K.	W/C
	21.8.18		Capt Woods rejoined from leave and attached to 15th D.A.H.Q as Adj. Staff Captain. 2nd Lt Stanaway rejoined from leave. 2nd Lt G Mitchell to W.Res. Lieut G.B. Page to 70 Bde RFA.	W/C
	22.8.18		Lieut Col Fergus Duncan D.S.O. Leave to U.K. 2nd Lt J. Stepham rejoined from Gas Course.	W/C
	26.8.18		S.A.A Section (detach) marched to BRAGUEMONT near NOEUX-les-Mines. Right Centre Sections at No 1 & 2 Sidoms to DAINVILLE WOOD. Captain H. Wigheman Lieut to U.K. (27.8.18)	W/C
	27.8.18		H.Q. No 1 & 2 Sidoms marched to AGNY.	W/C
AGNY.	28.8.18		"A" Echelon marched to WANCOURT area. 30/8/18 "B" Echelon marched to WANCOURT area.	W/C

CONFIDENTIAL.

WAR DIARY
=========

of

15th Divisional Ammunition Column.
_____

(Volume 21)

From 1st September 1918.   To 30th September 1918.

Army Form C. 2118.

WAR DIARY
or
INTELLIGENCE SUMMARY.
(Erase heading not required.)

Instructions regarding War Diaries and Intelligence Summaries are contained in F. S. Regs., Part II. and the Staff Manual respectively. Title pages will be prepared in manuscript.

15th. D.A.C.   September 1918

Place	Date	Hour	Summary of Events and Information	Remarks and references to Appendices
	1.9.18		2nd.Lieut ROWSELL F.S. struck off strength	
	1.9.18		Bombed by E.A. 1 Animals killed, 3 wounded, no casualties to personnel.	
	2.9.18		Lieut.V.C.HAMILTON struck off with effect from 29.8.18.	
	2.9.18		H.Q. and A.Echelon marched to FEUCHY Area.	
	4.9.18		Lieut.T.H.HARDMAN rejoined from leave.	
	5.9.18		Lieut.Col.J.Fergus DUNCAN granted extension of leave to 15.9.18.	
	5.9.18		Lieut.W.W.HADDOCK posted to 169 A.F.A.Brigade.	
	6.9.18		H.Q. and A.Echelon marched to West of ARRAS.	
	6.9.18		H.Q. and A.Echelon marched to LA COMTE.	
	7.9.18		Lieut.F.F.FINN posted from 71st.Brigade R.F.A.	
	9.9.18		H.Q. and 1 and 2 Sections marched to HERSIN. "B" Echelon rejoined and came under administration of D.A.C.	
	10.9.18		2nd.Lieut.F.W.GEDDES posted to 71st.Brigade R.F.A.	
			2nd.Lieut F.S.HIGHAM posted to 71st.Brigade R.F.A.	
	11.9.18		Following Officers joined from Base. 2nd.Lieut.W.G.SHARP, 2nd.Lieut.T.R.WALKER, 2nd.LIEUTH.J.PALMER.	
			2nd.LIEUT.W.M.ANDREWS, Lieut F.C.P.LEE, 2nd.Lieut.R.J.GIMBLETT.	
	12.9.18		2nd.Lieut.W.G.SHARP, and 2nd.Lieut.T.R.WALKER posted to 70th.Brigade R.F.A.	
			2nd.Lieut.H.J.PALMER, and 2nd.Lieut.W.M.ANDREWS posted to 71st.Brigade R.F.A.	
			Capt.W.LEAD granted leave to PARIS. Capt.G.R.RAWSON assumes Command.	
	15.9.18		Capt.A.R.WIGHTMAN rejoined from leave to U.K.	
	16.9.18		Capt.A.B.TAYLOR posted to 8th.Div.Arty.	
			Lieut.F.F.FINN granted leave to U.K.	
	17.9.18		2nd.Lieut.E.H.DURHAM rejoined from leave to U.K.	
	18.9.18		2nd.Lieut.A.T.JACK, 2nd.Lieut.J.BIRRELL and 2nd.Lieut.J.H.LOWE joined from Base.	
	18.9.18		2nd.Lieut.E.H.DURHAM, and Lieut.T.H.HARDMAN posted to 70th.Brigade R.F.A.	
			2nd.Lieut.F.BALDWIN struck off strength from 29.8.18.	
	23.9.18		Column marched to BARLIN.	
	24.9.18		Lieut.R.C.BAYLDON rejoined from leave to U.K. 2nd.Lieut.A.T.JACK posted to 70th. Brigade.R.F.A.	
	27.9.18		2nd.Lieut.J.H.LOWE attached to First Army Musketry Camp.	
	30.9.18		2nd.Lieut.J.BIRRELL posted to 55th.Div.Arty.	
			Capt.A.TAYLOR granted leave to U.K.	

Vol 37

CONFIDENTIAL.

War Diary

of

15TH D.A.C.

From 1/10/18 to 31/10/18

Volume 22.

Army Form C. 2118.

WAR DIARY
or
INTELLIGENCE SUMMARY.
(Erase heading not required.)

15th. Divisional Ammunition Column.

Instructions regarding War Diaries and Intelligence Summaries are contained in F.S. Regs., Part II. and the Staff Manual respectively. Title pages will be prepared in manuscript.

October 1918

Place	Date	Hour	Summary of Events and Information	Remarks and references to Appendices
BARLIN	3.10.18.		Lieut.F.F.FINN rejoined from leave to U.K.	M
-do-	4.10.18.		H.Q.& S.A.A.Section marched to BRACQUEMONT Nos.1 & 2 Sections marched to NOYELLES	
BRACQUE) MONT	7.10.18.		Lieut.Col.J.Fergus DUNCAN rejoined from leave to U.K.	M
	9.10.18.		2/Lieut. F. BALDWIN joined from Base.	
	10.10.18.		2/Lieut.J.B.CHILLINGWORTH joined from Base.	
	11.10.18.		Capt.G.R.RAWSON granted leave to U.K.	
	13.10.18.		2/Lieut.J.B.CHILLINGWORTH posted to 71st.Brigade R.F.A. Lieut.A.B.MARTIN and Capt.J.SPIERS granted leave to U.K.	
	16.10.18.		2/Lieut.F.BALDWIN posted to 15th.D.T.M.Brigade Lieut.Col.J.FERGUS DUNCAN assumes command of 15th.D.A.C. Capt.W.LEAD marched to FOSSE 7 near LOOS	M
FOSSE7 LOOS	17.10.18.		Headquarters marched to MEURCHIN. Nos.1,2,& S.A.A.Section marched to WINGLES.	
MEURCHIN	18.10.18.		Column marched to CARVIN	
CARVIN	19.10.18.		Column marched to WAHAGNIES.	
WAHAG- NIES	20.10.18.		Column marched to MERIGNIES.	
MERIGNIES	21.10.18.		Column marched to HUQUINVILLE.	
HUQUINVILLE	23.10.18.		S.A.A.Section marched to GENECH	
	24.10.18.		Major G.BUGLSTON BROWNE ,D.S.O., attached from 12th.D.A.C. assumes command of 15th.D.A.C. Capt.W.LEAD assumes command of No.2 Section.	
	25.10.18.		Headquarters,Nos.1 & 2 Sections marched to GENECH.	
GENECH	28.10.18.		Captain G.R.RAWSON rejoined from leave to U.K.	M
	29.10.18.		Captain J SPIERS and Lieut.A.B.MARTIN rejoined from leave to U.K.	

[signature] Captain R.F.A.
for Major R.F.A.

CONFIDENTIAL.

WAR DIARY.

of

15th Divisional Ammunition Column.

(Volume 23.).

From 1st November 1918.   To 30th November 1918.

WAR DIARY or INTELLIGENCE SUMMARY.

Army Form C. 2118.

15th Divisional Ammunition Column

November 1918

Place	Date	Hour	Summary of Events and Information	Remarks and references to Appendices
GENACH	1.11.18.		Captain A. TAYLOR struck off strength	
	4.11.18.		Captain W. READ posted to 70th Brigade R.F.A.	
	4.11.18.		Captain W. DONALD, M.C. joined from 70th Brigade R.F.A.	
	6.11.18.		2/Lieut. F. BALDWIN granted leave to U.K.	
	6.11.18.		2/Lieut. A. STANWAY admitted to hospital	
	6.11.18.		Re-organization of 15th D.A.C., New Establishment adopted, part European, part Indian.	
	8.11.18.		Headquarters marched to COBRIEUX	
COBRIEUX	9.11.18.		Column marched to LA GLANERIE	
LA GLANERIE	10.11.18.		Column marched to WEZ VELVAIN.	
WEZ VELVAIN	11.11.18.		Column marched to BAUGNIES.	
BAUGNIES	17.11.18.		Captain F.W. WHITEHEAD joined from 71st Brigade R.F.A.	
	19.11.18.		2/Lieut. W.A. COLQUHOUN posted to 71st Brigade R.F.A.	
	19.11.18.		2/Lieut. G. MITCHELL, D.C.M. joined from 71st Brigade R.F.A.	
	25.11.18.		2/Lieut. F. BALDWIN rejoined from leave to U.K.	
	27.11.18.		2/Lieut. F. BALDWIN joined from 15th D.T.M.Brigade.	

CONFIDENTIAL.

WAR DIARY

of

15th Divisional Ammunition Column.

(Volume 24.)

From 1st December 1918.   **To 31st December 1918.**

Army Form C. 2118.

WAR DIARY
or
INTELLIGENCE SUMMARY.

(Erase heading not required.)

15th. DIVISIONAL AMMUNITION COLUMN

DECEMBER 1918

Place	Date	Hour	Summary of Events and Information	Remarks and references to Appendices
GUI AU	1.12.18		2nd Lieut A.STANWAY Struck off strength.	
BAUGHIES.	8.12.18.		Lieut F.O.PALMER RFA, granted leave to BOULOGNE.	
	12.12.18.		No 78109. Sgt.E.PIERCY awarded MILITARY MEDAL.	
	15.12.19.		Column marched to TONGRE-NOTRE-DAME.	
TONGRE-N-D-	17.12.18.		Column marched to HORRUES.	
HORRUES	18.12.18.		Column marched to QUENAST.	
QUENAST	20.12.18.		Lieut R.C.BAYLDON. Granted leave to ROUEN.	
	27.12.18.		Major G.BUCKSTON BROWNE.D.S.O. granted leave to UNITED KINGDOM.	
			Captain LESLIE WOODS assumes command.	
			Captain W.DONALD.M.C. posted to 70th Brigade R.F.A.	

Woods.
Captain R.F.A.
Commanding 15th. D.A.C.

CONFIDENTIAL.

WAR DIARY.

of

15th Divisional Ammunition Column

(Volume 25)

From 1st January 1919.

To 31st January 1919.

Army Form C. 2118.

WAR DIARY
or
INTELLIGENCE SUMMARY.
(*Erase heading not required.*) 15th DIVISIONAL AMMUNITION COLUMN.

January 1919

Place	Date	Hour	Summary of Events and Information	Remarks and references to Appendices
QUENAST	1.1.19.		Lieut.Col.J.Fergus Duncan, leave to U.K. extended to 31.1.19.	
	6.1.19.		Major G.Buckston Browne died whilst on leave to U.K.	
	17.1.19.		2/Lieut. G.Mitchell, D.C.M. posted to 70th Brigade R.F.A.	
	19.1.19.		2/Lieut. F.Baldwin, to hospital for Dental treatment.	
			2/Lieut. J.H.Lowe granted leave to U.K.	
	23.1.19.		Captain F.W.Whitehead granted leave to BOULOGNE.	
	27.1.19.		R.S.M. Chatfield, C. to England for demobilization.	
	28.1.19.		Lieut: C.E.Hughes Davies joined from 15th Divisional Artillery Headquarters.	

CONFIDENTIAL.

WAR DIARY

of

15th Divisional Ammunition Column.

(Volume 26.)

From 1st February 1919.   To 28th February 1919.

Army Form C. 2118.

WAR DIARY
or
INTELLIGENCE SUMMARY.

(Erase heading not required.) 15th DIVISIONAL AMMUNITION COLUMN.

Place	Date	Hour	Summary of Events and Information	Remarks and references to Appendices
QUEMAST	2.2.19.		Lieut. W.W.EARLY joined from 15th Divisional Trench Mortars	
	2.2.19.		Lieut. I.SANDEMAN joined from 15th Divisional Trench Mortars	
	2.2.19.		Lieut. G.G.PAGE joined from 15th Divisional Trench Mortars	
	6.2.19.		Lieut. Col. J.FERGUS DUNCAN struck off strength	
	6.2.19.		Major G.BUCKSTON BROWNE struck off strength.	
	10.2.19.		2/Lieut. R.J.GIMBLETT evacuated to hospital	
	17.2.19.		Captain L.Woods evacuated to hospital	
	20.2.19.		2/Lieut. R.J.GIMBLETT, died at 1st Australian C.C.S. HAL, BELGIUM.	
	25.2.19.		Captain L.WOODS, died in hospital 1st Australian C.C.S., HAL, BELGIUM.	

CONFIDENTIAL.

WAR DIARY

of

15th Divisional Ammunition Column.

(Volume 27.).

From 1st March 1919.	To 31st March 1919.

Army Form C. 2118.

WAR DIARY
or
INTELLIGENCE SUMMARY.

(Erase heading not required.) 15th DIVISIONAL AMMUNITION COLUMN

March 1919

Place	Date	Hour	Summary of Events and Information	Remarks and references to Appendices
QUENAST	10.3.19.		Lieut.N.W.EARLY appointed Adjutant 15th D.A.C. vice the late Capt.L.WOODS.effect from 26.2.19.	adm
	12.3.19.		2nd Lieut. F.BALDWIN rejoined from hospital.	adm
	13.3.19.		Lieut. F.C.PALMER LEE granted leave to U.K.	adm
	20.3.19.		2nd Lieut. F.BALDWIN granted leave to U.K.	
	22.3.19.		Lieut. I.SANDEMAN proceeded to England for demobilization.	
	24.3.19.		2nd Lieut. J.H.LOWE transferred to 8th D.A.C. for duty.	
	26.3.19.		Captain A.R.WIGHTMAN, Medical Officer, posted to 70th Brigade R.F.A.	adm
	24.3.19.		Major V.LEAD rejoined 70th Brigade R.F.A. from temporary command of 15th D.A.C.	adm
	24.3.19.		Major V.BENNETT joined from 40th D.A.C. and assumes command of 15th D.A.C.	adm
	29.3.19.		Captain G.R.RAWSON granted leave to Paris.	adm
	31.3.19.		Lieut. J.C.OGILVIE granted leave to U.K.	adm
	31.3.19.		A/Captain N.W.EARLY proceeded to England for demobilization.	
	31.3.19.		Captain N.J.CAMPBELL, R.C.Chaplain proceeded to England for demobilization.	

CONFIDENTIAL.

WAR DIARY

of.

15th Divisional Ammunition Column

(Volume 28)

From 1st April 1919.   To 30th April 1919.

Army Form C. 2118.

WAR DIARY
or
INTELLIGENCE SUMMARY
(Erase heading not required.)

152 Divisional Ammunition Column

VOL 43

Instructions regarding War Diaries and Intelligence Summaries are contained in F. S. Regs., Part II. and the Staff Manual respectively. Title pages will be prepared in manuscript.

Place	Date	Hour	Summary of Events and Information	Remarks and references to Appendices
QUEVAST	8.4.19		Captain J Louse proceed to England for demobilisation.	Rut
	6.4.19		Lieut R B Brigham granted leave to United Kingdom	Rut
	9.4.19		Captain E Whitehead M.C. granted leave to United Kingdom	Army
	10.4.19		Major W Bennett posted to 1 Gordon Divisional Artillery	Rut
	10.4.19		Lieut L G Palmer posted to Gordon Divisional Artillery	Rut
	11.4.19		Captain G R Rawson assume command of 152 D.A.C	Rut
	12.4.19		2/Lieut L Baldwin rejoined from leave to United Kingdom	Rut
	15.4.19		Lieut A A Mallan granted leave to United Kingdom	Rut
	19.4.19		Lieut C B Page granted leave to United Kingdom	Rut
	20.4.19		Captain A R Wightman granted leave to United Kingdom	Rut
	24.4.19		Lieut J L Finn granted leave to United Kingdom	Rut
	28.4.19		Lieut J C Ogilvie rejoined from leave to United Kingdom	Rut

R W Robertson
Lieut R.F.A.

Army Form C. 2118.

WAR DIARY
or
INTELLIGENCE SUMMARY.
15th Divisional Ammunition Column

(Erase heading not required.) May 1919

Vol 44

Place	Date	Hour	Summary of Events and Information	Remarks and references to Appendices
QUENAST	3-5-19		2/Lieut. J Allison posted to 8th Divisional Artillery	(yo)
	4-5-19		Lieut. J.E. Ogilvie posted to "O" Strong Bank	(yo)
	7-5-19		Capt. J.W. Whitehead M.C. proceeded to England for demobilization	(yo)
			Capt. B.E. Hughes Games proceeded to England for demobilization	(yo)
	10-5-19		Capt. G.R. Rawson granted leave to U.K.	(yo)
	14-5-19		Lieut. J J Finn proceeded to England for demobilization	(yo)
	30-5-19		Lieut. A.B. Marlew proceeded to England for up our arm	(yo)

E. N. Durham Lt. Col
Durham Lt.Col

www.ingramcontent.com/pod-product-compliance
Lightning Source LLC
Chambersburg PA
CBHW081547160426
43191CB00011B/1859